When you ask what a university means, you ask what your own children mean, and what the American future means. You ask, by inference, the deepest personal question: What sort of human being am I? ... Symbols of the fitting answer shine before us: a University, an imperishable flame set alight by Bowman Ashe; a beacon glowing brighter as Jay Pearson adds lustre to its faculty, expands the shining architecture of its physical plant and brings forth new dreams that could be made bright reality. This light — this University, increasingly irradiates and so erases gloomy ignorance, dark corners of poverty, Stygian pockets of superstition and fear. There is no question of its value to us.

Philip Wylie, in "The First 30 Years of the University of Miami," 1957

There are times when cities take off. There are times when universities take off. When those times coincide, there is the stuff of combustible excitement. We are here at the threshold of such times.

President Edward T. Foote, inaugural address, December 4, 1981

UNIVERSITY OF Miami

GREAT SEAL UNIVERSITY OF MIAMI · CORAL GABLES · FLORIDA 1925

PHOTOGRAPHED BY BRIAN SMITH

HARMONY HOUSE
PUBLISHERS LOUISVILLE

Executive Editors: William Butler and William Strode
Library of Congress Catalog Number: 87- 083169
Hardcover International Standard Book Number: 0-916509-34-6
Printed in Canada by D.W. Friesen through Four Colour Imports
First Edition printed Fall 1988 by Harmony House Publishers,
P.O. Box 90, Prospect, Kentucky 40059 (502)228-2010 / 228-4446
Copyright © 1988 by Harmony House Publishers
Photographs copyright © 1988 Brian Smith

Thanks for photography help goes to Bob Callahan, Dennis Copeland,
Rich Dalrymple, Gayle Holden, Richard Lewis, Steve Rice, Sally
Stapleton, Laura Weinsoff and *The Miami Herald*.

INTRODUCTION

The University of Miami and its South Florida metropolitan area grew up together, each helping foster the development of the other. Miami and its university were built by energetic, visionary people who found magic in the beauty of the area. Miami of the 1920s was a place where bold plans could blossom, nourished by the exchange of ideas that occurs where cultures, commerce, peoples, and customs mix freely. Situated at the crossroads of two hemispheres, Miami of the 1980s is still such a place and today the University of Miami is the largest private university in the Southeast.

For many years the University of Miami was the only major university serving the southern half of the state. Though it has always been private and independent, it responded to the public's needs. Through its doors have passed most of the doctors, lawyers, judges, teachers, architects, engineers, nurses, musicians, accountants, and scientists who helped guide the growth of South Florida. Even as the University of Miami grows to international stature, it will continue to serve the people of its community.

Likewise, the community is responsive to the University's needs. In 1984 the Board of Trustees of the University launched a fund-raising effort to propel the institution to the front ranks of American higher education.

The goal to raise $400 million in five years was the second largest effort ever undertaken in the nation. It is a measure of the power and progress of this university that the ambitious campaign goal was surpassed 21 months early.

From its quiet beginning just over six decades ago, the University of Miami has risen through uncommon commitment of its leaders, its faculty, and its community to become internationally known for scholarship and research. Throughout the University there is a sense of achievement, energy, and promise.

The Coral Gables campus, which is the heart of the University, is characterized by tropical beauty that sets this university apart. The excitement of discovery is shared by scholars, students, and researchers working in a variety of disciplines in both basic and applied research. Research into the causes and cures for such diseases as diabetes, Alzheimer's disease, and cancer are conducted on the medical campus, one of the busiest and best medical centers in the nation. Faculty and students working just a few miles away on the waterfront campus of the Rosenstiel School of Marine and Atmospheric Science study ocean currents, track the weather, and seek solutions to preserve our oceans.

Any university with such a wide variety of programs has many faces. The many faces of the University of Miami reflect a special place rapidly becoming one of the finest institutions of higher education in the nation.

A UNIVERSITY OF MIAMI CHRONOLOGY

1925 A charter of incorporation for the University of Miami is obtained; the Board of Regents announces the Coral Gables location, in response to George Merrick's offer of 160 acres and $5 million, to be matched from other sources.

1926 The University opens the "Cardboard College," offering a liberal arts and music curriculum; Bowman Foster Ashe is elected president of the University.

1928 The School of Law opens.

1929 Aviation courses begin; Schools of Business Administration and Education open.

1934 President Ashe purchases the assets of the University at auction.

1939 The San Sebastian Hotel is purchased for an administration building and women's dormitory.

1940 Accreditation is granted by the Southern Association of Colleges

1941 The Graduate School opens, offering degrees in English, botany and zoology.

1943 F.G. Walton Smith establishes and serves as director of the Marine Laboratory.

1945 Dr. Ashe announces plans for a new campus to be built on the original site; Veterans enroll in large numbers.

1946 Winston Churchill accepts an honorary degree of Doctor of Laws at an academic convocation in the Orange Bowl.

1947 The School of Engineering is created. Arts and Sciences adds a major in radio, followed by a major in radio/television.

1952 The University opens the state's first School of Medicine; Construction begins on a medical school building; Jackson Memorial Hospital is designated as the teaching hospital of the School of Medicine.

1953 Jay F.W. Pearson is appointed president.

1956 Baron de Hirsch Meyer provides the funding for new School of Law facilities.

1962 The Board of Trustees elects the third president, Henry King Stanford.

1968 The School of Nursing is established.

1969 The Institute for Marine Science becomes the Rosenstiel School of Marine and Atmospheric Science.

1971 The Mailman Center for Child Development is constructed.

1973 The division of Continuing Studies is formally established as the School of Continuing Studies.

1976 The five-year Mid-Century Campaign is launched with a goal of $129 million. The goal is exceeded six months ahead of schedule.

1981 Edward T. Foote II is inaugurated as the fourth president.

1983 The School of Architecture and the Graduate School of International Studies and its research center, the North-South Center, are created; the Hurricane football team wins the national championship, defeating Nebraska 31-30 in the Orange Bowl.

1984. The $400 million Campaign for the University of Miami is announced; the first and only residential college in the southeast opens.

1985 The School of Communication is established.

1986 The Board of Trustees approves a new comprehensive campus master plan for the Coral Gables campus.

1988 The Hurricane football team wins second national championship, defeating Oklahoma 20-14 in the Orange Bowl; The Campaign for the University of Miami surpasses its $400 million goal 20 months ahead of schedule.

The whole dramatic and remarkable development of the University thus far permits only one interpretation — that we have a rendezvous with greatness...keeping that rendezvous should be the motivation that stirs our minds and our energies in the years ahead.

President Henry King Stanford, in "Rendezvous with Greatness," 1972

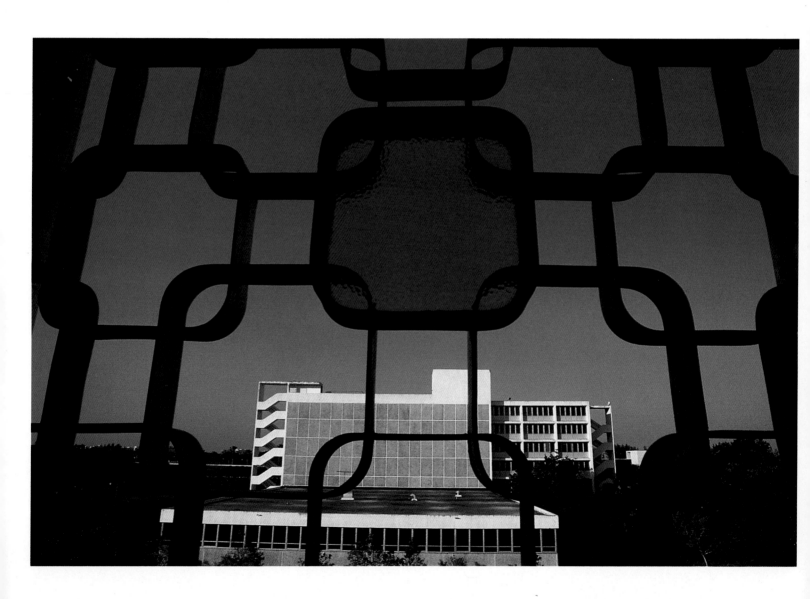

No one can overestimate the value of this University to the state and to the entire south, in the opinion of nearly everyone in the Miami district. It will be a cultural center for the south, and its trained minds will have an enormous influence on the taste and cultural values of this entire region.

Coral Gables *Bulletin*, June, 1925

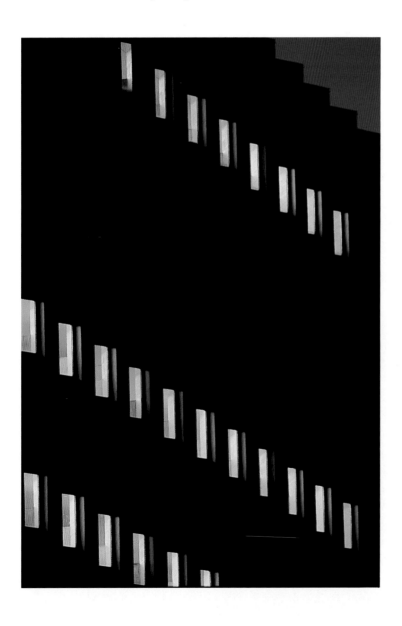

The campus is located in the heart of the best residential section of Coral Gables, a 160 acre panorama of glorious tropical beauty. The administration building, a triumph in architecture, is mirrored in the quiet lake just a stone's throw away. Hibiscus, bouganvillea, oleanders, and poinsettias flank winding pathways and walks shaded by rows of stately Royal Palms... So we have here in this wonderful climate amid ideal surroundings a great institution of learning which inspires and fosters the spirit of tolerance, high ideals, and good fellowship extending to the four corners of the earth.

The Ibis, first edition, 1927

An independent, comprehensive university requires of its faculty more than teaching, although in teaching the university regenerates its institutional soul. It requires research and creativity. The role of the faculty must remain absolutely central, because individually and collectively, the faculty — the teachers, the scholars, the creators — is the essence of a university.

President Edward T. Foote, inaugural address, December 4, 1981

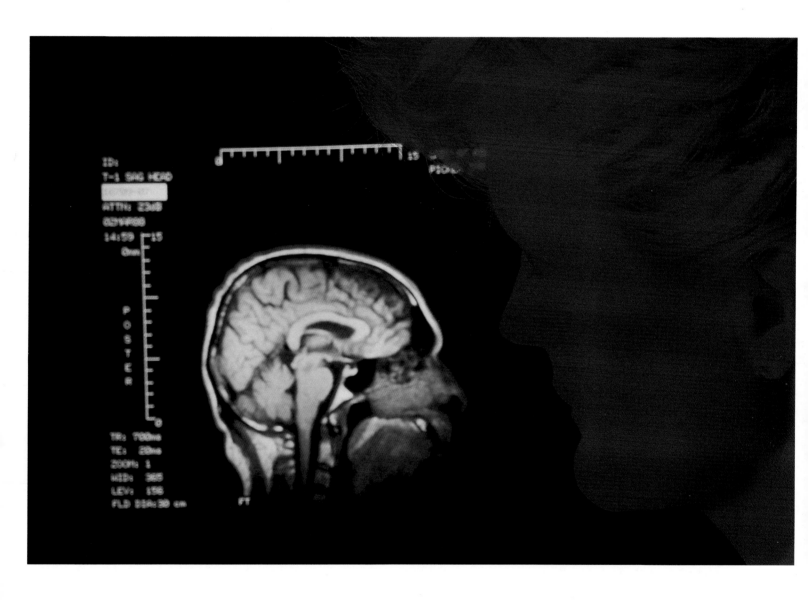

41

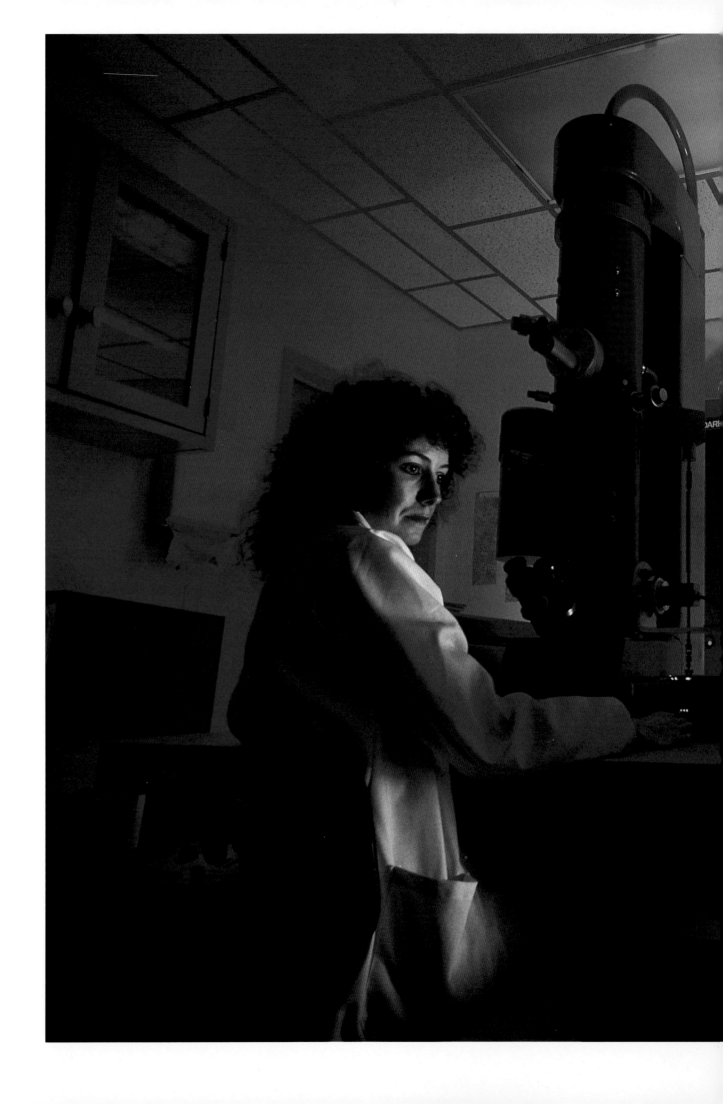

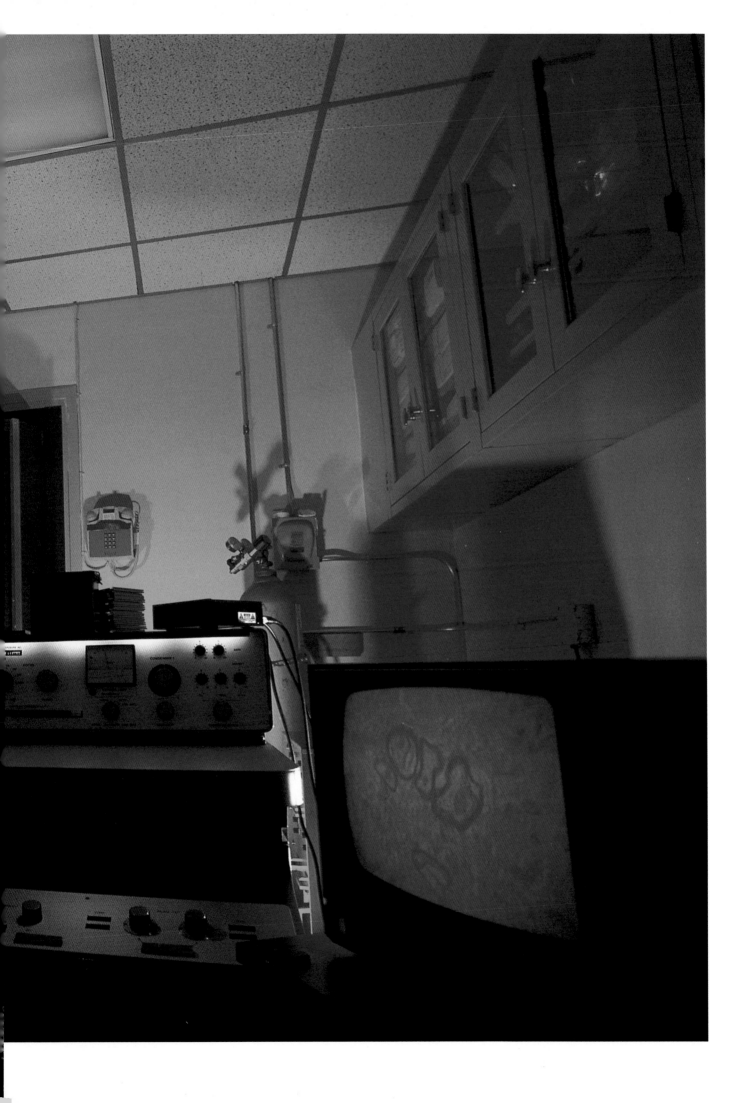

The true university has a responsibility to serve and contribute to the society in which it lives...It also has an obligation to man's intellectual and cultural tradition, transcendant of time, place, politics and society. It is a trustee of the legacy of civilization.

President Henry King Stanford in "A Report to the Board of Trustees," 1964

45

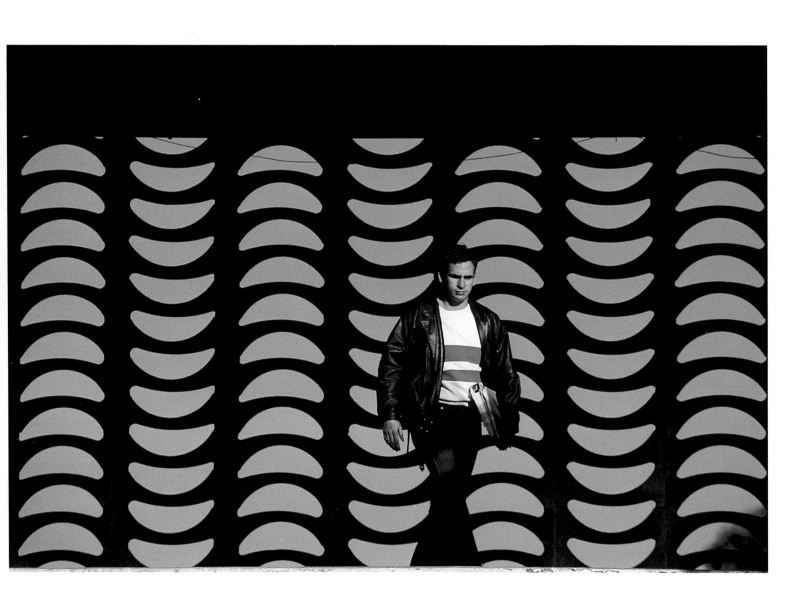

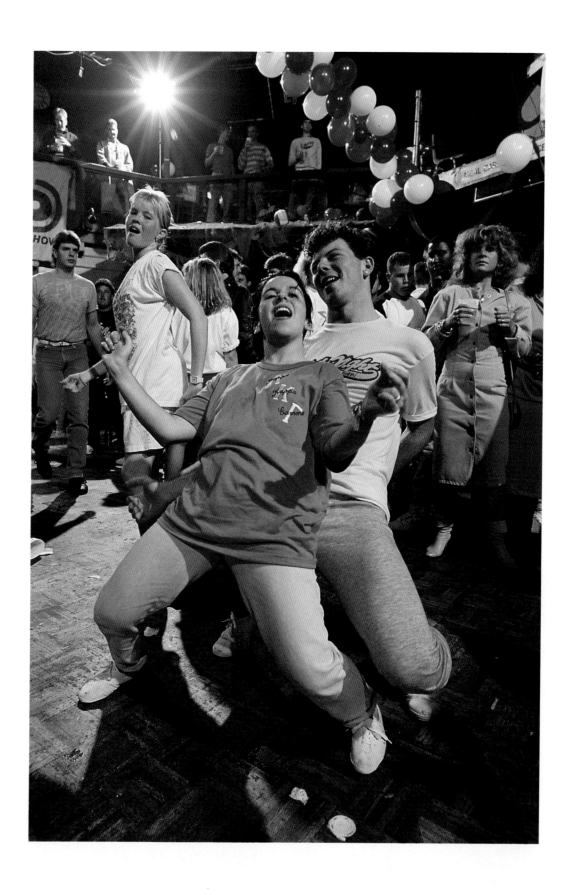

A young school as schools go, Miami has capitalized upon its youth. There are no centuries-old traditions to fetter the imagination. There is a glow of youth across the campus, a youth-fulness of spirit, a vitality, of excitement for the institution and its growing potential for becoming one of the national centers of academic life.

From *Barron's Profiles of American Colleges,* 1973

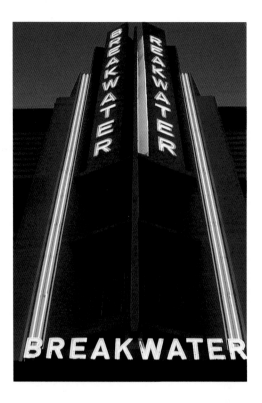

The University of Miami has come of age with Greater Miami...In no other place in the world have more marvels been wrought in such a short space of time than have been brought into being in Greater Miami. Nowhere else could dreams equal to ours, at our University, be dreamed with the confidence that soon, perhaps very soon, they may become a reality.

President Jay F.W. Pearson in *The Future's Challenge to the University of Miami,* 1957

The University of Miami...is a phenomenon which needs some interpretive mementos. It is big. It has a bouncy vitality. The subtropical setting involves more than the mere fact that ivy won't grow on its walls. Strange dream-like things happen to it. An alligator decimates the white ducks in its campus lake. It fields a polo team which in four years of intercollegiate play is never beaten. The unregarded football team shoots meteoric to the level of the rarer stars. Nationally important research develops from these ideas skill-fully caught with shoestring lassoes. It cannot all be laid to chance.

The University of Miami — The First 25 Years, 1951

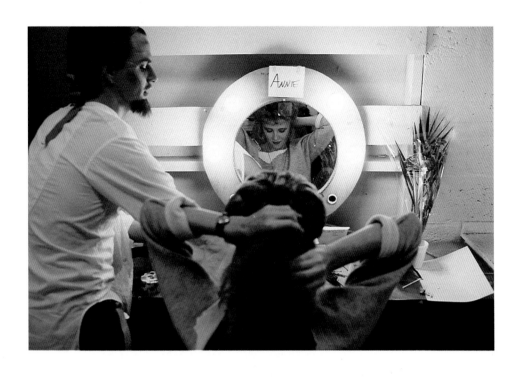

I see a university in which its tropical location nurtures emphasis on the physical world in our backyard, even as we try to comprehend all the rest of it. Thus, we should strive to become preeminent in the tropical branches of such sciences as botany, zoology, medicine, and oceanography.

President Edward T. Foote, inaugural address, December 4, 1981

"Siempe Arriba" is as valid a direction signal for our University today as it ever was. This concept does not mean continuous, easy ascent. Upward thrust in the University's history has always been accompanied, and brought about, by struggle. But the battle today is not for survival, but for distinction. It is, however, a battle no less worth waging and winning.

President Henry King Stanford, "Report from the President," 1979-80

Since October, 1926, when the first students took their seats in the "cardboard college" and looked askance at the flimsy walls, the University of Miami has had lots of hard knocks. Somehow we have kept going. Maybe we have learned to roll with the punches. More likely, the truth inherent in a University and the power of human hope are why we survived hurricanes, wars, booms, and the scarcity of dollars... Each graduating class is another revelation of the University of Miami's destiny. Unheard-of achievements are ahead. Exciting new adventures, in learning and doing are waiting. Greatness beckons to you and your Alma Mater.

President Bowman Foster Ashe, Silver Anniversary address, 1951

What is next? What can be next following such a prologue and anticipating such uncertainty in a future so charged with promise and danger? What if anything can be predictable in the midst of such change, such riptides in the human condition? And how should a university of tomorrow in a city of tomorrow respond today? The beginning of that answer is to keep asking the question, simply to keep asking how we who would do the good work of teaching, learning and discovering can do it better. The day we stop asking, the day we are content with our present knowledge, will be the day our work as an intellectual community atrophies.

President Edward T. Foote, 60th anniversary convocation, 1986

Southern sun and sky-blue water
Smile upon you, Alma Mater;
Mistress of this fruitful land,
With all knowledge at your hand,
Always just, to honor true,
All our love we pledge to you.
Alma Mater, stand forever,
On Biscayne's wondrous shore.

Alma Mater by William Lampe
and Christine Asdurian

THE
VOYAGES
Of
The Ever Renowned
Sr. FRANCIS DRAKE
Into the
WEST INDIES.
Viz.
His great Adventures for Gold,
and Silver, with the Gaining thereof, and
an Account of his Surprising of Nombre
de Dios.
A large Account of that Voyage wherein
he Encompassed the World.
His Voyage made with Francis Knollis, and
others; their taking the Towns of St. Jago,
Sancto Domingo, Carthagena, and Saint
Augustin.
His last Voyage (in which he Died) being
Accompanied with several Valiant Com-
manders, and the Manner of his Burial.
Collected out of the Notes of the most Aproved
Authors.
which is added, An Account of his Valo-
Exploits in the Spanish Invasion.
LONDON,
Thomas Malthus, at the Sign of the Sun,
the Poultry, 1683.

HISTOIRE
DE LA
FLORIDE.
PREMIERE PARTIE.
LIVRE PREMIER.
Dessein de l'Auteur. Bornes de la Floride.
qui elle a été découverte. Coûtumes de ses Ha-
bitans. Préparatifs de Ferdinand de Soto pour
en faire la conquête.

CHAPITRE I.
Dessein de l'Auteur.
J'ai dessein d'écrire la decouverte
la Floride, & les actions mer-
bles qui s'y sont passées
comme Ferdinand de
cuta de grandes ch...
Tom. I.

PAG. I

Groundbreaking for the University
of Miami in 1926. Left to right are
Phineas Paist, Denman Fink,
Frederick Zeigen, Mrs. Zeigen
and Bertha M. Foster.

Founder and benefactor George E. Merrick speaks to an enthusiastic crowd
at the cornerstone-laying of the University of Miami, February 4, 1926.

It all began here with an optimistic crowd of UM enthusiasts and
curious Coral Gables residents at the cornerstone-laying, 1926.

In October, 1926, the University of Miami opened, one month behind schedule and heavily in debt, in the unfinished Anastasia Building, nicknamed the "Cardboard College."

The first faculty of the University of Miami, assembled here in April, 1926.

The "Cardboard College" under renovation, 1926-27.

This skeleton of the original Merrick Building, 1945. The 1926 huricane and financial misfortune had halted construction on the site. In 1945 President Ashe announced plans to rebuild the University on this site, after a gift of land from Grace Doherty completes the 245-acre tract. The building, modified to a more modern design, opened in 1949.

In 1939 the San Sebastian Hotel is purchased by the University for administrative offices and a women's dormitory.

Groundbreaking for the new School of Law, opened in 1928.

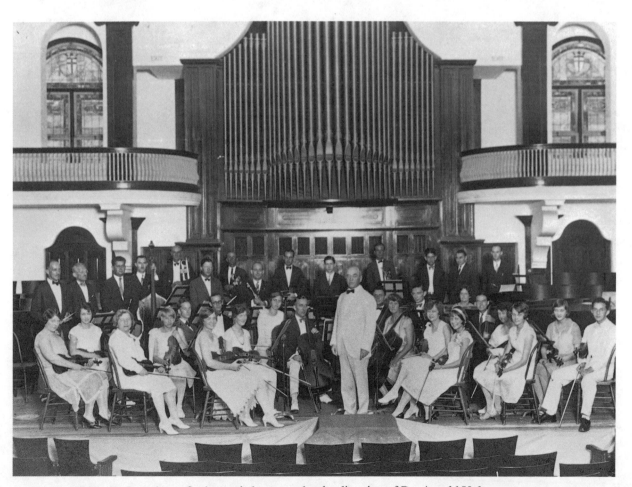

In 1927, the Symphony Orchestra is begun under the direction of Dr. Arnold Volpe.

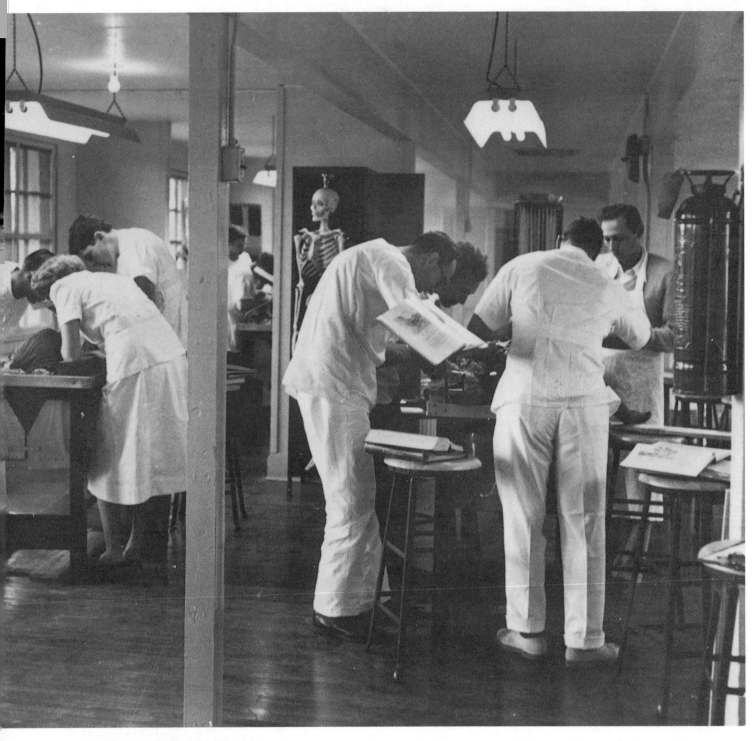

In 1952, the University opened
Florida's first School of Medicine.
Students began their classes in a
building in Coral Gables, leased
from the Veteran's Administration
on the site of the Biltmore Hotel. In
December, 1953, Jackson Memorial Hospital was designated the
teaching hospital of the School of
Medicine.

In March, 1941, trainees from the Royal Air Force arrive in Miami to begin navigation training. The Duke of Windsor visits Miami and his troops during the war years.

In 1940, the University, in conjunction with Pan American Airways, began a program to train cadets in air navigation and meteorology for the U.S. Army Air Corps.

In 1946, Winston Churchill received an honorary Doctor of Laws degree from the University during an academic convocation at the Orange Bowl, February, 1946. President Ashe accompanies Mr. Churchill to the ceremony.

In 1948 polo begins as an intercollegiate sport, and Miami wins the national championship four years in a row.

Mike Fiore of the Hurricane baseball team. Miami has been national champion twice, in 1982 and 1985

Miami's swimming and diving teams have produced 82 All-Americans over the years, and women's national championships in 1974 and 1975.

1981 U.S. Amateur champion Nathaniel Crosby of the Hurricane golf team. The men's team has qualified for the NCAA championships six out of the last seven years. The women's team has been national champion in 1970, 1972, 1977, 1978 and 1984, with five individual national chamions and two U.S. Amateur champions. *Photo by Caryn Levy.*

Susana Rojas and Elizabeth Levinson of the Hurricane tennis team, 1986. Miami's team won the NCAA doubles championship in 1986, and had the NCAA singles runner-up in 1975.

The University's football teams in the early days (shown here in 1934) were very competitive, with wins in the 1935 and 1946 Orange Bowls.

The 1946 football team beats Holy Cross 13-6 in the Orange Bowl.

Miami has been the national football champion twice, in 1983 with coach Howard Schnellenberger, and 1987 with coach Jimmy Johnson. Here place-kicker Greg Cox gets three points for the 'Canes.

Mike Irvin hauls in a pass for the Hurricanes. Miami football teams have appeared in fourteen post-season bowl games since 1935, and in every year since 1984. *Photo by Micki and Richard Lewis.*